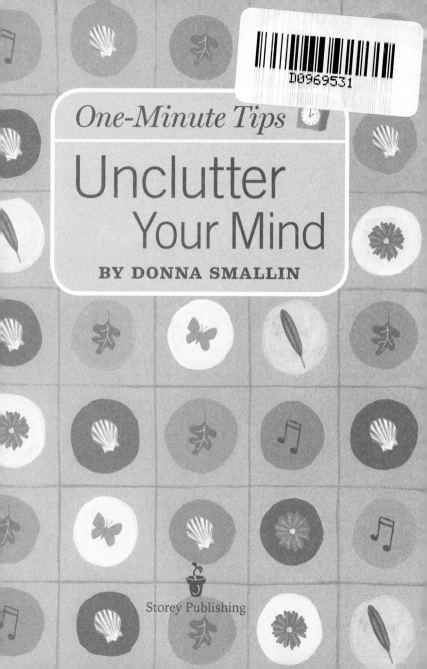

One-Minute Tips

Unclutter Your Mind

BY DONNA SMALLIN

Storey Publishing

*The mission of Storey Publishing is to serve our customers
by publishing practical information that encourages personal
independence in harmony with the environment.*

Edited by Nancy D. Wood and Rebekah Boyd-Owens
Cover design and art direction by Mary Velgos
Cover and interior illustrations © 2006 by Juliette Borda
Cover photograph © by David Schmidt
Text production by Jennifer Jepson Smith, based on design
    by Wendy Palitz
Indexed by Diane Brenner

© 2006 by Donna Smallin
A previous version of this book was published as
    7 Simple Steps to Unclutter Your Life, 2000.

    The information in this book is true and complete to the best of our knowl-
edge. All recommendations are made without guarantee on the part of the author
or Storey Publishing. The author and publisher disclaim any liability in connection
with the use of this information. For additional information please contact Storey
Publishing, 210 MASS MoCA Way, North Adams, MA 01247.
    Storey books are available for special premium and promotional uses and for
customized editions. For further information, please call (800) 793-9396.

Printed in the United States by CJK
10 9 8 7 6 5 4 3 2

Library of Congress Cataloging-in-Publication Data
Smallin, Donna, 1960–
    The one-minute organizer to unclutter your mind / Donna Smallin.
        p. cm.
    Includes index.
    ISBN 13: 978-1-58017-636-1; ISBN 10: 1-58017-636-4 (pbk. : alk. paper)
    1. Self-management (Psychology) 2. Time management.
I. Title.
BF632.S63 2006
646.7—dc22
                                                    2006018177

For Mom and Dad,
who turned out all right after all.

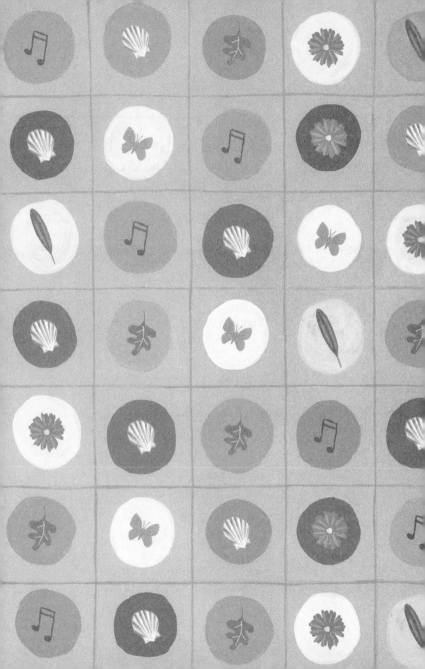

contents

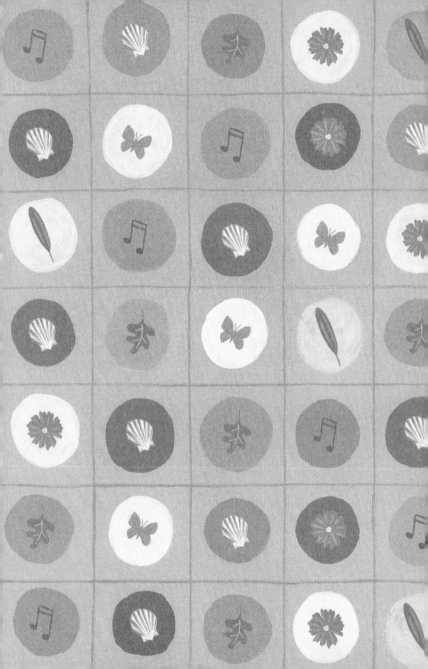

introduction

There have been many times in my life when I wanted to scream, "Stop the world — I want to get off!" What I really wanted was to stop time, so that I could catch up on everything that was making demands on me.

I used to make long lists of things to do and, like everyone who writes lists, I enjoyed the satisfaction of crossing off each task as I completed it. But the list was endless. There was always too much to do and too little time.

Not only did I never have enough time, I never had enough money. I earned a decent income, but the money went out as quickly as it came in — sometimes faster. I felt like I was working for nothing.

Then, I took a five-day bicycle trip that changed my life. It was my first vacation in four years. I rode between

40 and 70 miles each day. Occasionally, other cyclists accompanied me, but mostly I rode alone. The trip gave me plenty of time to think.

One day, it dawned on me what was wrong with my life. I had been "pedaling along," not realizing that I was lost. I was not living true to myself or to my values. I wasn't even sure who I was anymore. I just knew I was unhappy.

I was unhappy because I had made some bad choices — about how I spent my time, money, and energy — and I was living with the consequences of those choices. Thankfully, I realized that I didn't have to live with those consequences forever. With the support of friends and family, I found the courage to make new choices.

I share this with you to make an important point. If there's something that's not working in your life, only you can make it right. That's what this book is all about: making your life right again. *Because you deserve to be happy.*

Simplicity, One Moment at a Time

Something made you pick up this book. Does it feel as if your life is spinning out of control? Are you feeling stressed out? Lost? Unhappy? Do you wish you had more time to spend with family and friends? More time to enjoy life? Less debt? More savings? Or are you feeling so confused and helpless that you don't know who you are or what you want?

What you'll find in *One-Minute Tips: Unclutter Your Mind* are hundreds of practical tips and ideas for uncluttering your busy mind and improving the quality of your life. It is the premier busy person's guide to clearing away daily worries, stresses, and behaviors that gunk up the works. Where clutter now lives, self-awareness, joy, delicious silence, and authentic laughter can be fostered.

This book is divided into two parts: Clear Out and Keep Clear. Chapters include strategies for moving from a place of overload to a place of focused connectedness. Each page offers practical advice for any day of the week, any time of the day. Every tip can be read in seconds; many implemented in as little as one minute. Look for the one-minute symbol ①.

I promise you this: If you put even a fraction of these tips into practice, you will begin to create a simpler, happier, more satisfying life *immediately.*

PART ONE

Clear Out

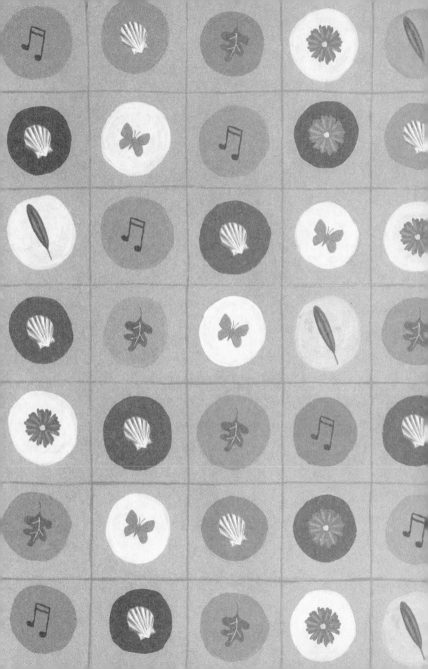

CHAPTER 1

Be Here Now

Mindfulness is about waking up, living in the present, and making conscious choices about what you do, say, and think. Choosing well — in every moment — takes constant watchfulness. But it is time well spent.

In the "busyness" of living, it's easy to lose ourselves as well as the precious moments of our lives. How quickly the present becomes the past! When you concentrate on being fully present in the moment, the moments accumulate over months and years into a life well lived.

be here now

☀ Don't just do something, sit there! Take time now to look at what's going on around you. What do you see and hear? What do you feel? **Stopping** every once in a while makes you more aware of what you are doing when you start moving again.

☀ Worry about right now. If you find yourself worrying about something that might happen tomorrow or some day, concentrate on today. Take it one day at a time. And if that's too much to think about, take it one hour at a time.

be here now

Trying to keep your attention focused on the **here and now** requires that you continuously remember to be aware of your focus. Use your breathing to help you do this. Tune into each breath — feel it — without feeling the need to change how you are breathing. In becoming more aware of your breathing, you become more connected with the here and now.

❶ Repeat to yourself as often as needed each day: Where am I? Here. What time is it? Now. Leave the past behind. When your mind is cluttered with past experiences, especially negative ones, it drains energy and productivity from today.

be here now

① Focus on the **task at hand.** Whether you are washing dishes, driving to the store, doing your job, or helping your children with homework, focus all of your attention and energy on what you are doing right now.

It's not easy to "stop and smell the roses." We've trained ourselves to always be thinking ahead. But if you never live in and FULLY ENJOY the present, what kind of life are you living?

be here now

Watch your every move. Over the next week, before you do anything, ask yourself why you are doing it. Is it important? Is it important enough to do right now?

A ringing telephone is a perfect example. Most people automatically answer the phone without deciding to answer it. It's there for our convenience, but how easy it is to become enslaved by it!

be here now

☀ Slow down. Practice awareness. Try this simple exercise: Stand up and deliberately move across the room in slow motion. Notice how it increases your **awareness** and expands time. That's what slowing down in life can do for you.

How much of what you do is action and how much is reaction? By **paying closer attention** to what you are doing, you can make more conscious choices about how you spend your time.

be here now

Take a hike. A long stroll is the perfect opportunity to reflect on what's happening in the world and in your life.

Set your own **goals.** Think about what you want in life and what you need to do to make your life the way you want it. Write down your goals as they occur to you. Cross off your list any goals that are imposed on you by someone else.

be here now

① Listen to your **thoughts.** Don't judge them; just recognize and accept them.

① How often do you think or say, "I have to"? Replace this statement with "I choose to." It will relieve a lot of the pressure you place on yourself.

Many times, we focus our attention on trivial matters to avoid dealing with larger, more important issues. A preoccupation with keeping a spotless house, for example, may be masking a communication problem in your marriage.

Eating mindfully is a part of living mindfully. Make it a point to sit down when you eat. When eating, be aware of each mouthful of food. Notice the texture as well as the taste. Chew slowly, **savoring** the flavor. Put down your fork between each mouthful.

Focusing on eating allows us to more fully enjoy our food and aids proper digestion. In addition, eating slowly gives your stomach time to register the feeling of fullness, which reduces the tendency to overeat.

be here now

Know your emotions. Crying doesn't always mean you're sad. Sometimes we cry out of joy. Or we cry out of anger and frustration. And sometimes we take out our anger on innocent people and things.

Ask yourself at regular intervals throughout the day: How am I **feeling?** What do I need? If you're reacting because you're tired, take a nap. If you want to unwind, call a friend. If you're stressed out, do some deep breathing.

be here now

A lot of stress can be traced to the negative "chatter" in our minds — muddled thoughts about what we said or did, should have said or done, or what we think we might say or do — which distracts us from fully enjoying the present. **Meditation** provides a welcome break from external and internal noise and chaos.

be here now

Try this meditation exercise:

1. Sit quietly in a chair and gently close your eyes. Be aware of your breath as it flows in and out of your body. Is it shallow or deep? Is your inhale longer, shorter, or the same as your exhale? Just notice these things without changing them.

2. Pay attention to bodily sensations — the feel of your breath in your nostrils, your lungs, and your belly.

3. Allow yourself to experience whatever feelings come up. If stray thoughts about the past or future enter your mind, exhale them with your next breath and return to your breathing and this moment.

4. Do this for 5 minutes and try to work up to 15 to 20 minutes in one sitting.

be here now

Relationships are one of the most important components of our lives. Why is it that we barely spend a moment thinking about them? Are you taking the time to reflect on the health of your relationships? Don't wait for signs of trouble before you start paying attention. **Nurture your relationships** with friends, family, and coworkers. Start today.

be here now

Actions speak louder than words. What do your actions tell your friends? What do their **actions** tell you?

-🔆- ❶ Recognize that we're all doing the best we can. If there is someone in your family or office with whom you frequently become frustrated, tell yourself the next time you interact with that person that he or she is doing the best he or she can at this moment in life. Notice how that belief eliminates much — if not all — of your frustration with this person.

When did you last chat with your best friend or hug your sister? It's so easy to get caught up in doing that we often don't MAKE TIME to be with the people we care about most.

be here now

☀ ❶ Keep in touch. Buy a bunch of cards or keep a pack of **postcards** handy to send when the mood strikes. E-mail cards are also a great way to surprise a friend. Check out www.bluemountain.com, where you can select and send an e-mail card for just about any occasion — for free. Getting an unexpected card or letter in the mail can really brighten up the day for a friend.

Give that which you most wish to receive. If you want love and respect, show **love and respect.** If you want forgiveness, forgive yourself and others.

be here now

Recognize that you cannot change other people. If someone you care about has a problem, don't make it your problem. **Just listen** and be there.

Attack the behavior, not the person. If someone's behavior is upsetting to you, make a **simple statement** such as, "When you [do whatever it is he or she is doing], I feel [whatever it is you are feeling]," and then wait for a response. While their first instinct may be to defend themselves, very often when people learn that their behavior is causing someone undue stress, they will want to change that behavior, especially if they value the relationship.

be here now

1 Hold the advice. People often complain about things that are going on in their lives, but they're not necessarily looking for solutions — just an ear. Make it a point to give out advice only when specifically asked.

If you feel you must give unsolicited advice, **be gentle.** Always include a positive statement with a negative statement. If a friend tries to give you advice you didn't want to hear, try to remember that your friend is doing so because he or she cares about you.

BE YOURSELF

and allow others

to be who they are.

be here now

If it's hard to make time to go out to dinner or a movie with a friend, try inviting a very close friend to go grocery shopping with you. Even a short drive to and from your destination gives you a chance to catch up and feel more a part of each other's lives.

As you change, your relationships will **change.** Often, this change requires a period of adjustment. But not every relationship can withstand change. Some relationships are able to exist only under certain conditions. It's okay to end a friendship that's not working out. If the relationship is not mutually satisfying, it is no longer a friendship.

be here now

☀ If you want to get to know someone, **ask questions.** People like to talk about themselves. Don't you?

☀ Be quick to give thanks. Also, be quick to say, "I'm sorry."

☀ **Face conflict** head-on. Conflict is a normal aspect of everyday life. When you find yourself in a dispute with someone, invite that person to be your ally in finding a solution. Say, "Okay, it appears that we have a conflict. What can we do about it?"

be here now

Listen and learn. When listening, make a conscious effort to let go of memory, desire, and judgment. For the moments you are listening, exist only as **an ear connected to a heart.**

☀ Watch people. Nonverbal communication accounts for 93 percent of communication. To hear the whole message, maintain eye contact and observe facial expressions, hand gestures, and body movement.

The love of another is something we all wish to have throughout our lives. A **loving relationship** makes you feel happy, secure, and content, as well as confident in the feeling that you are worthy of love. But, as we all know, a loving relationship is not easy to maintain, and, in fact, requires a lot of care and work.

Know what you want from a love relationship before entering it.

be here now

An authentic love relationship requires that both parties know what they want out of it and **communicate** this to each other. It is not about one person giving up everything else for the other.

In *Live Your Dream*, author Joyce Chapman suggests that you ask yourself the following questions:

Does my current relationship support me in living my dream?

What's working in my relationship?

Are my needs and desires known and important in our relationship?

be here now

☀️ **❶** Surprise your mate every once in a while. Write "I love you" in toothpaste on the mirror, make his or her favorite meal, offer to give a foot massage. Or write a note that expresses your appreciation for a specific personal quality or recent action and pin it to his or her pillow.

be here now

Allow relationships to grow and change. Consider yourself and those you love as **works in progress.**

Think about what kind of partners you want to be. How do you want to treat each other? Write a succinct statement that sums up your answers. For example: "Our mission is to support each other as we strive to achieve our individual **dreams.** We do this because we believe that it will bring us closer together in body, mind, and spirit."

be here now

If you are waiting for a loved one to figure out what you might like, be prepared to wait a very long time. No one knows what you want unless you ask for it. Keep requests simple and **straightforward,** and include a time frame, if possible. For example, "Could you please call me as soon as you know that you are going to be running late?" Rehearse your request until you can ask for what you want without anger, criticism, or whining.

❶ Make the effort to listen to — and remember — what your mate tells you about his or her day-to-day life, hopes, and dreams.

be here now

Make and keep a regular weekly date. Set aside time for just the two of you — without distractions like the telephone, pager, and television, and without the kids. Go to your favorite restaurant. Take a walk or a hike. Go to an outdoor concert or festival. Make it a date that lets you **connect** physically, socially, intellectually, spiritually, emotionally, and romantically.

Enjoy **simple pleasures** together. Entice your partner outside in the evening. Sit side-by-side on the porch steps and listen to crickets, watch fireflies, or gaze at the stars.

1 Get touchy. If a picture paints a thousand words, then a touch speaks volumes about the depth of your affection. **Touch** can also melt defenses. If you feel a fight coming on, reach out and touch your significant other. Face each other and hold both hands as you express feelings of hurt or anger.

Get away. **Rekindle** passion with a change of scenery. Book a room at a romantic inn or a nice hotel near home. Let your spouse in on the plan — or make it a surprise!

be here now

Family relationships, like love relationships, need a great deal of attention to keep everyone happy. Sometimes this attention might take the form of a specific action, such as a group vacation or outing, while at other times all you need to do is evaluate the health of your **family relationships.** Be mindful of yourself and the rest of your family, and you will be able to fully enjoy the good times as well as help each other through the bad times.

be here now

Leave stress at work. Studies have shown that if Mom or Dad comes home grumpy from work, the stress and negative emotions can infect the whole family like chicken pox. If you've had a bad day, do something on the way home to improve your mood. Listen to **soothing** music in your car or take a brisk walk.

Plan one-on-one time with your children. Ask children to take turns helping you to prepare dinner. They might balk at first, but will soon begin to look forward to their turn if, during your time together, you shower them with attention. Ask about school, friends, favorite subjects, and dreams.

Appreciate your children for WHO THEY ARE instead of who you want them to be.

Fathers: Be mindful. According to a research study at Oxford University in England, fathers who spend as little as five minutes a day talking with their sons help to boost their child's **self-esteem** and self-confidence. Talk about their problems, their schoolwork, and their social lives. Do the same for your daughters.

be here now

Plan weekly **family time.** Schedule at least one morning, afternoon, evening, or day every week that provides an opportunity for all family members to have fun together. Take turns making suggestions about what to do next.

Studies have shown that men and women alike attribute their emotional state (whether they're happy or depressed) to relationships within the family. If you are unhappy, look at your feelings about your **family life.** What isn't working for you? What is within your power to change?

Express your feelings in a non-aggressive way with a statement that focuses on those feelings. Example: "I feel that the time I spend cooking meals goes unappreciated" versus "You never thank me for making a nice dinner."

be here now

You might wish sometimes that you had more time or energy to give your children. And from time to time, you might want to kick yourself for something you said or did. But if your children feel safe, wanted, and **loved,** that's what really matters.

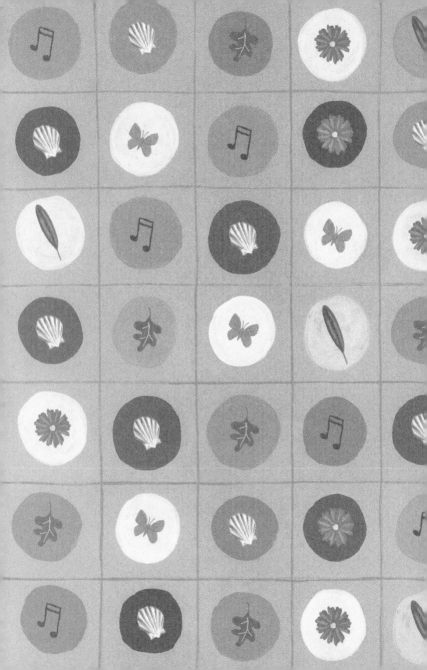

CHAPTER 2

Choose Authenticity

To make emotionally rewarding, authentic choices in life, you must know who you are and what's important to you. People who are face-to-face with death learn quickly what's important. But you don't have to wait for a crisis to figure out what really matters. Do it now.

When you choose to live according to your values, you will have more time, less stress, and a sense of personal freedom. And that is what uncluttering your life is all about.

choose authenticity

So often we make choices without thinking about what our needs are, or do things in a particular way because that's the way we learned to do it. We do things our usual way and we never question our motives.

To **live authentically,** you must ask yourself: Am I doing things *my* way, for my own reasons, or because that's what everyone else is doing?

choose authenticity

Most of us are moving so quickly each day that we don't stop to think about where we are going or what we are doing. But stopping and thinking can change your life.

Take a personal retreat in which you devote a few hours or even a day or two — perhaps with a few friends — to talk about how you want to spend your **time here** on earth. Ask your friends and yourself: If you were to die tomorrow, what would you like to be remembered for? What personal qualities? What achievements?

choose authenticity

Don't take on anything new right now. Plan to spend some time getting to **know yourself.** Who are you? What do your choices in life (career, home, car, clothes, and friends) say about you? Is that who you really are? For example, if it didn't matter what anyone else thought about what kind of car you drive, what kind would you choose?

If you BELIEVE that what other people say or think about you matters, ask yourself why.

choose authenticity

❶ Ask yourself, "Who am I?" Try to base your answer on who you are *right now*. Can you do it? Our perceptions of ourselves are often clouded by past experiences and future assumptions that can prevent us from discovering who we really are.

What would you like to have more of in your life and why? What would you like to have less of and why? **What motivates you?** Is it money? Is it time? When you know what motivates you, you can build motivators into your life as a reward for achieving milestones.

choose authenticity

What do you value? According to Joyce Chapman in *Live Your Dream*, to determine **what's important** to you, look at the life you are living now and answer the following questions:

What do you find yourself doing most often?

How do you spend your time?

What do you talk about?

What do you do when you have a day off?

What offends your sense of justice and provokes outrage in you?

Which of your values are you most proud of?

choose authenticity

Remember that **life is a journey,** not a destination. What do you hope to accomplish in your life? Is what you're doing now helping you to achieve your goals? What would be your ideal day? Your ideal week? Your ideal year? What do your answers tell you about yourself?

You are in the driver's seat. WHERE would you like to go NEXT?

choose authenticity

Make a list of the **qualities** you admire and respect in yourself and others. Honesty, resourcefulness, intelligence, style, and simplicity are just a few examples. Identify your values by noticing how you spend your time and money and why those are your choices.

Imagine that you have only a short time to live. In *Live Your Dream,* Joyce Chapman suggests this exercise: Think back over the past month. How would you spend your time differently? How would **your priorities** change? What would become more (or less) important to you?

choose authenticity

Become aware of what you believe. **Positive beliefs** drive positive behaviors; negative beliefs drive negative behaviors. If you are unhappy with your behavior, try to determine what belief is prompting it, and then take the necessary steps to replace that belief with a more positive one.

For example, if you want to lose weight because your clothes are getting uncomfortable, but you don't change your eating or exercise habits, perhaps you believe deep down that you don't deserve to feel good. To change your behavior, you've got to change that belief.

choose authenticity

❶ Recognize that change is a natural process of life. Like every other creature on earth, we have the ability to adapt ourselves to our environment. We can choose to make positive **changes** in ourselves that will improve our quality of life. Being conscious about our choices (rather than simply reacting to circumstances) and following through with them makes a commitment to ourselves.

Allow TIME to change. Focus on the PROCESS of changing rather than the outcome of change. Be patient.

choose authenticity

Choose **one value** or quality or characteristic you would like to develop — or eliminate. List all the ways you can think of to do that. Start doing one of these things today.

In *Live the Life You Love,* Barbara Sher advises us to gather our **allies.** She suggests creating a team of imaginary spirit allies: for example, a person in history, someone from your childhood, a fictional character. Imagine what advice they would give if you asked for their support.

choose authenticity

1 Just *don't* do it. If the reason you continue to do something is that you've been doing it for a while and feel it would be time and energy wasted to stop now, **think** again. Think about what you have gained and how you have grown through your investment of time, energy, and money.

Now think about the time, energy, or money you are wasting by continuing to do something because you feel obligated. Think, too, about all the things you could be doing but can't do because of this obligation. If you are unhappy, unfulfilled, or unsatisfied, give yourself permission to leave this thing behind and **move on.**

❶ Give it a **try.** Be willing to try something new to see how it works. If you keep doing things the same way, you'll keep getting the same results.

❶ Commit to your goal. The moment you fully **commit** to a goal is the moment when that goal begins to be a reality. Without full commitment, a goal is just a goal.

choose authenticity

Once you've determined your true beliefs and values, you are ready to put them into action. Don't be afraid to let the world see who you really are. When you "be yourself," you give others **permission** to do the same. With no false fronts to keep up, life is so much simpler and more satisfying.

Start by developing a vision statement. A **vision statement** is a statement about what you want to be and what you want to achieve or contribute. Take some time to develop it. Write it down. Keep it where you will see it frequently. Read it aloud. Often.

choose authenticity

Make a list of things that make you **happy.** Write them as they occur to you or as you notice your enjoyment in an activity. Challenge yourself to come up with at least 100 ideas. Then resolve to do at least three of those things each day for the next three weeks.

choose authenticity

If you **believe** that you are a capable, talented person, then you will become that person. If you believe that people are helpful, you will find yourself in the company of helpful people. What you believe about yourself and your life will become true. You might feel that you are only acting or pretending, but faking it is the easiest way to change your life. Fake it until you can make it.

-☀- Hold mental rehearsals. **Visualize** yourself reaching your goal, or visualize yourself going through the steps to reach that goal.

① Write several **affirmations** and post them somewhere as a reminder to say them aloud every day. An affirmation is a positive statement that often begins with the words *I will* or *I can* or *I am.* An example of an affirmation for a cancer patient is: "I can feel myself growing healthier and stronger each day."

Find quotes or sayings or posters with messages that **inspire** you to be and do your best. Place them where you will see them every day.

choose authenticity

❶ Eliminate the words *should* and *have to* from your vocabulary and your mind. Replace them with "want" and "choose to." If you don't believe that you want to do something, then why are you doing it?

Once you are aware of your values, **consciously choose** to inject them into your life. For example, if you value integrity, make only those promises you can keep — and keep them.

Take 10 minutes each day to reflect how you will (or did) align your expenditures of time, energy, and money with your values throughout the day.

When you let someone else make choices for you, you are giving up the POWER to make yourself happy.

choose authenticity

Live with **no regrets.** If you were to die tomorrow, what would you regret not having done? How can you live your life today (and every day) so that you will have no regrets?

-☀- ❶ Be gentle with yourself. If you find yourself slipping back into old patterns, congratulate yourself for recognizing that! Then **reclaim** your will and move on.

choose authenticity

Everything in moderation — that's the secret to happiness and good health, right? Right. But it's difficult to maintain **balance** in our lives because it takes great concentration and effort.

How do you know when your life is in balance? You know you're on the right track when you function well even when life is difficult, not just when life is running smoothly. Balanced, your overall satisfaction with life remains the same regardless of the rockiness of the ride.

choose authenticity

❶ Bring balance to your life by **focusing attention** where attention is needed. The next time you feel angry, frustrated, guilty, resentful, or stressed, note whether the feeling is a reaction to home issues, career issues, or focused on leisure time. Do you frequently feel this way about this area of your life? If so, resolve to bring your attention to this area and make an effort to make some changes that will bring balance into your life.

choose authenticity

Are you a hard worker or a workaholic? The difference between them is **state of mind.** Working hard to achieve a goal is admirable. Workaholics work for the sake of working, believing that it will somehow make them worthier.

❶ Imagine life as a game in which you are juggling five balls. Name them: work, family, health, friends, spirit. Work is a rubber ball; if you drop it, it will **bounce back.** But the other four balls — family, health, friends, and spirit — are made of glass. If you drop one of these, it might be irrevocably damaged.

choose authenticity

If your life is a whirlwind of activity seven days a week, try balancing it with some **true leisure time** — a time to just sit — without feeling the need to be productive or busy doing something. Let yourself stop and rest. Spend less time talking about your need to relax and more time doing it. It will refresh your spirit and make you more efficient when you return to your responsibilities.

When you are with
your family, give them
100 percent of your
ATTENTION and
energy. When you are
at work, engage fully in
your job. And when you
are playing, have fun!

choose authenticity

If you work particularly long and hard one day or if you feel exhausted, make a conscious effort to take it a little easier the next day. Sleep later. Go out to lunch with a friend. Leave work a half hour early. Squeeze in a nap. Or do nothing at all. The key is to relax and **recharge.**

choose authenticity

To give yourself a time-out, try this relaxing and refreshing exercise:

1. Put on some relaxing music and lie comfortably on your back.

2. Take deep breaths in, and slowly let them out. Focus on each inhalation and exhalation. Relax into each breath.

3. Relax your feet. Imagine that they are growing very heavy. Then let the feeling of heaviness spread very slowly through your body. Even your face feels heavy, as if gravity is pulling it down into the floor.

4. Just lie there, enjoying the stillness and the quiet.

5. After 20 minutes, deepen your breaths and begin to stretch. Roll onto one side for a minute, and then sit up slowly.

choose authenticity

If you've been swamped with dead-lines, spend a whole day with no plans. Just do what you feel like doing, when you feel like doing it. If you have to make a lot of decisions at work, give yourself a time-out: Let someone else decide where to go, what to do, and what to eat. If your job requires constant contact with people, escape into solitude. Go for a walk in the woods or paddle a canoe on a quiet lake.

choose authenticity

If you wish you had **more time** for your family, then make more time. Where there's a will, there's a way.

If you have a tendency to drive faster than the speed limit, get in the habit of allowing an additional 5 to 10 minutes of driving time. You'll be not only less stressed, but safer too.

Plan to do something you love to do every day — anything from playing solitaire on your computer to reading or drawing to walking the dog.

1 Detach yourself slightly from your environment. Use this as a technique for becoming more objective about your role at home and work. As a more objective observer, you are more likely to find ways to improve your **balance.**

Schedule time for **fun.** At the beginning of each month, put "fun stuff to do" on your calendar to balance the demands and responsibilities of home and career. Include family events as well as things that will give you private time.

Don't try to plan every minute of your time. Leave time to do WHATEVER you feel like doing at the moment, which may be nothing at all.

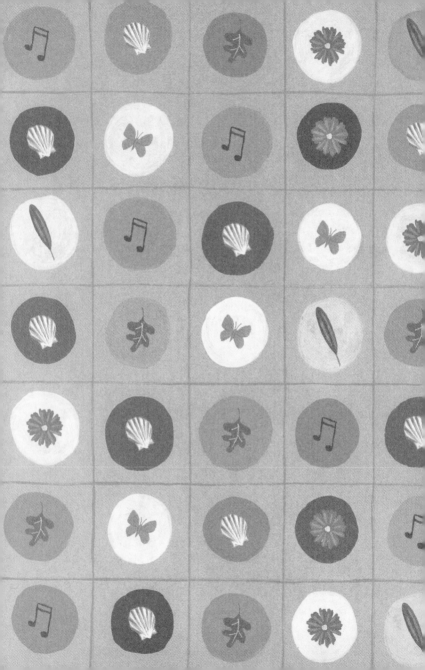

CHAPTER 3

Focus Inward

It's not easy juggling the demands of family and career along with your own needs. Some days we accomplish extraordinary things and even manage to keep everyone happy. But at what cost? We're stressed out, tired, and even a little angry.

Often, we sacrifice our own plans and goals to meet the needs of others. Or we don't even *make* plans and goals for ourselves because we figure, "Why bother?" If you want to unclutter your life, choose to put yourself first.

focus inward

Choosing to put yourself first is not being selfish; it's being self-caring. There's a big difference. **Caring for yourself** — physically, emotionally, intellectually, socially, and spiritually — will make you happier, healthier, and better able to cope with the demands of daily living. In fact, by putting your own needs first and reserving even just a little more time and energy for yourself, you will have more to give to others.

focus inward

No matter how valiantly we try, we **can't do everything** all of the time. And we can't do some things as often or as well as we would like to do them. So we wind up feeling like we've failed somehow. Yes, family is important. Yes, work is important. And yes, there's only so much time in a day. But if you don't take care of your own needs, who will?

focus inward

Wouldn't it be wonderful if we could **stop time** long enough to get caught up? Well, maybe someday time travel will allow us to do just that. But time is not the real issue. It's how we choose to spend our precious time that determines how fulfilling our lives are.

Somewhere along the way, we got into the habit of going, going, going all the time. We've been doing it for so long, we rarely stop to think about what we're doing and if it really matters. We just get up each morning and get on life's treadmill. Why?

As long as everyone else is racing through life at warp speed, we feel compelled to keep up. But if the pace is getting too intense, we can choose to SLOW DOWN.

focus inward

☀ Do **one special thing** for yourself today. Buy yourself a bouquet of flowers, paint your toenails, or simply go outside tonight and wish upon a star.

focus inward

☀ 1 Before you go to bed tonight, start a list of things you've been putting off — things you would like to do if you had the time.

☀ 1 In the morning when you get dressed, make a point to wear **something you love,** like a favorite sweater, scarf, or piece of jewelry. Throughout the day, every time you catch a glimpse of yourself in a mirror, think of one thing you would really love to do and say to yourself, "I make time for other things. I can make time for this too."

focus inward

① So often, we want and need help but don't ask. **Asking for help** is not a sign of weakness; it takes courage to ask for help. Once you admit to needing help, you may find that it comes from the most unexpected sources.

Perception is reality. If you feel like you're overwhelmed, you are overwhelmed. But you can regain some control over your life. And now is just as good a time as any.

focus inward

Document your day. In your diary or on a sheet of notebook paper, jot down everything you do from the time you wake up until the time you go to bed. Try to account for every hour. Do this every day for a full week. At the end of the week, take a look at how you spent your time. Then determine where you can **cut back** to free up some "you" time.

① Schedule "you" time into your daily planner and keep your appointment.

focus inward

Commit to putting yourself first for three weeks. Don't let anyone or anything interfere with your time. Really give it your **best effort.** If you're concerned about taking time away from other people and things, remind yourself that it's only for three weeks. At the end of that time, ask yourself what, if anything, you lost and what you gained. In all likelihood, the gain will outweigh the loss.

focus inward

Keep a **journal.** Jot down what you've done for yourself each day. How did it make you feel? How did your family, friends, boss, and colleagues react? If you weren't able to keep your appointment with yourself, describe why. What happened? How can you prevent it from interfering with your time in the future?

Create a positive self-image. ACT as if you are a person with an EXTRAORDINARY ability to nurture and care for yourself, and you will become that person.

focus inward

Give yourself the **gift** of 15 minutes each day to do something you really enjoy. Get up 15 minutes earlier if you have to, but try to carve it out of your existing day. This is not the time to clean house or prepare the kids' lunches; it's your time to do something for you.

Whether you're a couch potato or an athlete, your body needs fuel to function. If you **feel** like taking a nap after lunch or you crave sweets and carbohydrates, your body is telling you something: The fuel you're giving it is insufficient for the demands of your daily life.

focus inward

Follow these simple guidelines for a well-balanced diet:

- Eat raw fruits and vegetables, beans, nuts, and seeds.

- Choose whole grains over processed grains in pasta, breads, and cereals.

- Eat two fruits or vegetables at each meal.

- Eat modest servings daily of fish, chicken, turkey, lean beef, or pork. Vegetarians, eat adequate protein from legumes.

- Choose skim milk over whole milk, and low-fat cheeses over regular cheeses.

- Eat fruit, bagels, or English muffins instead of doughnuts, cakes, and cookies.

- Go light on butter, margarine, oils, sugar, salt, and alcohol.

focus inward

Don't eat too much. Eat three meals a day, but stick with one regular-sized helping at each meal. You can eat a light snack between meals if you get hungry.

Don't eat too little. Calories equal **energy.** You need a certain number of calories just to get you through your day. Even if you're trying to lose weight, you should still eat three meals a day. Consuming too few calories can cause your body to enter a protective state in which your metabolism slows down and begins to store fat because it thinks you're starving!

focus inward

Don't skip breakfast. Eating a healthy breakfast provides fuel for your **mind and body.**

When shopping for groceries, spend more time around the perimeter of the store, where you'll find fruits, vegetables, breads, fish, meats and dairy products. With the exception of cereals, grains, pastas, herbs, and some frozen foods, the inner aisles in a grocery store contain mostly processed or junk foods. Shop with a list and buy only what's on your list.

focus inward

One of the best ways to take care of yourself is to maintain a healthy weight, which may mean shedding a few pounds. And there's only one way to do it: For every pound you want to lose, you've got to "lose" 3,600 calories by either consuming 3,600 fewer calories or burning them off.

Reaching and maintaining a **healthy weight** can be a life-long battle. But it's a battle that's well worth the fight, especially if you spend a lot of time or energy worrying about your weight, or if you don't feel good about yourself because of your weight.

focus inward

If you are more than 10 percent over your healthy weight, aim for one to two pounds of weight loss per week.

If you **walk** at a moderate pace for 30 minutes every day, eat sensibly, and cut out a couple of desserts a week, you could lose about one pound in a week.

Avoid fad diets, especially diets that severely restrict caloric intake or entire groups of foods. You may lose weight quickly following one fad or another, but quick weight loss is usually followed by quick weight gain.

focus inward

-☀- Make **small changes.** If you simply replace one 8-ounce glass of soda a day with water, you could lose 10 pounds in a year.

Remember that all foods are okay to eat — but not okay to eat at all times. When you are tempted to eat gooey chocolate cake or a big bag of potato chips, try saying, "I'm not going to eat this today because right now I'm trying to eat **healthier foods.** I can have that some other time." Recognizing that these foods are not forbidden forever makes it easier to turn them down for now.

focus inward

A glass of juice is a healthier choice than a glass of soda, but it has about the same amount of calories. **Water** is always the best choice. Coffee has zero calories, but the calories in sugar and creamer add up fast. Try nonfat creamer.

Don't let being self-conscious about your body get in the way of participating in activities you enjoy, such as swimming, dancing, and cycling. You have the right to enjoy **any activities** regardless of your body shape or size. Remember that your self-esteem and identity come from within.

focus inward

-☀- **➊** Remind yourself to **be patient.**
Allow yourself time to achieve your
healthy weight. Once you get going,
weight loss adds up fast. Do the
math: A loss of 1 pound a week adds
up to 52 pounds in a year!

focus inward

Eating less for dinner is one way to shave off a few hundred calories each day. The key is to decrease your **appetite.** Try eating a healthy midafternoon snack. Exercise for 30 to 60 minutes just prior to your evening meal. Drink a large glass of water before sitting down to eat, or eat a salad before your main course.

❶ Read labels. You don't have to read everything on the label, but do look at serving size, fat, and calories.

focus inward

If you eat right and exercise but can't seem to reach your **ideal** body weight, don't panic. First, consult with your physician to make sure there aren't any underlying problems. If everything checks out okay, relax. It's probable that your "ideal" is based on the media's idealistic — often unrealistic — body image.

A single workout can boost your energy, lift your spirits, and make you feel great.

In addition to helping to control weight, **regular exercise** over time can combat anxiety and depression, improve self-esteem, and help you better manage stress.

focus inward

Engage in 30 minutes of moderate exercise every day.

Begin with 10 to 15 minutes of exercise a day at a **comfortable** pace. Over a period of a few weeks, gradually increase the length of your workout to 30 minutes or more each day. Then work on increasing your pace so that you can hear yourself breathing and feel your pulse quicken.

Choose an exercise you enjoy — and one that you can work into your schedule. Walking is ideal because it can be done anywhere, by just about anyone.

focus inward

-☀- Get out and exercise even when you don't feel like going. Notice how you are feeling at the halfway point. More than likely, you'll be glad you made the **extra effort** to get out.

Break it up. To improve fitness, you'll want to strive for 30 minutes of exercise three to five times a week, but it doesn't have to be 30 consecutive minutes. Any physical activity that gets your heart beating faster counts toward the 30-minute goal.

focus inward

Rediscover the **joy of playing!** If the word *workout* keeps you from exercising, think of it as playtime. Try doing some of the things you used to do as a kid. Remember how much fun you had? Go for a bike ride. Walk to a friend's house. Swim at the community center pool. Or take a hike in the woods and pretend it's an adventure!

focus inward

When you and your kids enjoy a special treat like ice cream, follow it up with a 10-minute walk. It's a great way to spend **quality time** with your kids.

There are lots of events that rely on walkers, runners, and cyclists to raise money for a cause. An event like this is a **great motivator** to get you into the swing.

❶ Make plans to walk, jog, cycle, dance, swim, or skate with a friend or group. Not only will you enjoy it more, but you'll be more motivated to keep it up as well.

Honor your goal to be healthy, but don't fret if you never lose that last 10 pounds. You are still a BEAUTIFUL person with the POTENTIAL to achieve a happy, healthy, successful life.

focus inward

If **walking** is your exercise of choice, pump your arms as you walk to increase the intensity of your workout. You can burn even more calories in a shorter time by walking hills.

Dancing is a great way to get in a workout and have fun. Maybe you can interest your partner in **dance** lessons — or have a little fun with your kids. Put on some music and try to dance through three to five songs. Let them choose the music one day and you choose the next.

If you're CRUNCHED for time or not motivated to exercise, tell yourself that you're just going to do half today. Once you get going you may want to KEEP GOING.

focus inward

Taking the time to eat well and exercise is the single best way to stay healthy. And being healthy makes you feel good about yourself. In fact, developing a healthy lifestyle can give you a whole new perspective on life. When practicing **wellness,** you may find that the things that used to stress you out don't seem so stressful anymore.

1 Strive to treat your body with **respect.** Give it enough rest. Fuel it with a variety of foods. Exercise it appropriately, and listen to what it needs.

focus inward

Smoking adds wrinkles around your eyes and mouth, stains your teeth, and makes your clothes and everything in your house dirty. It also increases your risk of heart attack, stroke, and lung and throat cancer. When you **quit smoking,** these risks eventually return to almost that of a nonsmoker. Don't wait until it's too late; do what you have to do now to quit.

Find a doctor who is a good listener. You will be more apt to share your concerns and thereby alleviate unnecessary fears.

focus inward

Celebrate wellness! Let your birthday be a reminder each year to schedule an annual physical exam. **Regular checkups** can help to catch potential health problems before they become serious. Taking better care of yourself now will help you live longer, with fewer disabilities and health problems.

focus inward

Soap and water are the best prevention against germs that can cause colds. Forget the antibacterial soap; any soap will do. For best results, **wash your hands** like nurses do: for a full 60 seconds.

The simple prescription for many minor (and some major) illnesses is regular, moderate exercise. Whether you suffer from depression or varicose veins, high blood pressure or high cholesterol, hemorrhoids, or menopausal hot flashes, a 30-minute walk four or five times a week can **work wonders.**

focus inward

Sufficient water consumption helps all of your vital organs function better. Lack of fluid intake can result in fatigue, weakness, listlessness, sore muscles, jitters, and even the blues. A good rule is to drink twice as much water as it takes to quench your thirst.

Water keeps your skin smooth and **healthy.** It helps minimize cellulite and wrinkles. And it can help to prevent common illnesses and medical problems. Drinking water flushes toxins out of the body. It also can help you lose weight because you feel more full.

focus inward

Following are some tips for drinking more water:

- Drink water while you're waiting for your coffee to perk.

- Take a bottle of water with you when you leave the house.

- Never pass a water fountain without stopping to drink.

- Drink water before — and during — every meal.

- Keep a pitcher of water in the refrigerator at all times.

Isn't it time you did

SOMETHING NICE

for yourself?

focus inward

If you've had a bad day, come home and take a shower or bath and wash your worries away.

Give yourself a pedicure. Soak your feet for 10 to 15 minutes in a dishpan filled with warm water and bubble bath. Dry feet thoroughly. Use a pumice stone to remove calluses. Trim your toenails straight across and gently push back cuticles with a cuticle stick. To **refresh** feet, massage in peppermint foot cream. Apply nail polish for a finishing touch.

Go to a spa-a-a-h. Leave your worries at the door and enjoy a little bit of **heaven on earth.**

focus inward

A quality-time session with your significant other should be more than a once-in-a-while occasion. Invest some time and energy in preparing for a **romantic interlude** with your partner. Make a reservation at your favorite restaurant or plan a romantic dinner at home with candlelight and music. Think of ways to make it an evening to remember. Planning is half the fun!

Buy sexy lingerie. No one sees what you're wearing under your business suit or casual attire, but if it's something sexy, it makes you feel sexy, and that's a treat in itself!

focus inward

Tough day at work? Pick up a movie and something to eat on your way home or have dinner delivered.

Love to cook? Cook yourself a **gourmet** meal. By taking the time to prepare yourself a nice meal, you are saying, "I'm worth it."

Indulge your craving for chocolate. Don't worry; a little bit of chocolate once in a while is not going to kill you. In fact, chocolate contains antioxidants similar to those in red wine, so it may help you live longer!

SPLURGE on a fantasy.

focus inward

☀️ Listen to music. Turn off the television and enjoy whatever is **music** to your ears. Put on your favorite CD or go outside and listen to the sounds of nature.

☀️ Call a good friend and plan a night out with no kids and no spouses.

Pack a bag and **retreat** to your favorite destination. Or go visit a friend or family member whose company you really enjoy.

focus inward

Take a **wellness day.** Using a paid personal day or an unpaid day off, tell your boss you don't need a sick day but you do need a wellness day to help prevent you from getting sick! Then do whatever your heart desires on that day.

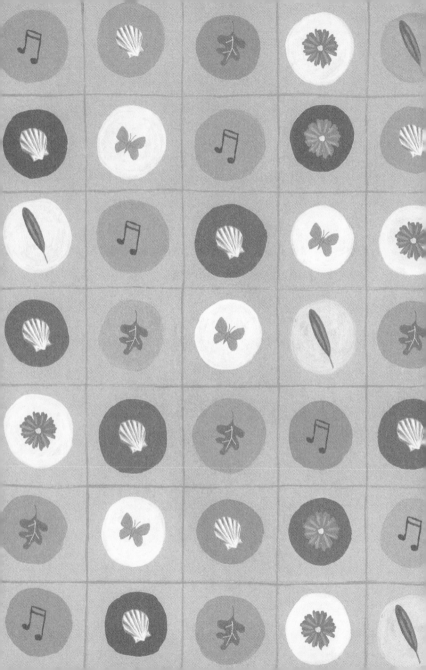

CHAPTER 4

Find Your Center

It's not easy to live simply in our complex world. But truly, life is as simple or as complicated as we make it. We can scurry here and there, or we can slow down and stop to enjoy the simpler pleasures — most of which can be found in our own homes and backyards. If you want to live a simpler life, the secret is to string together a series of simpler days. That means making new choices about how you spend your time and energy.

find your center

Get into "wash and wear." Go through your clothes closets and drawers, and **pull out** clothes that require special care, such as dry cleaning or ironing. Consider giving them away. Buy clothes that are machine washable and do not need ironing.

Wear a **natural** hairstyle. If you have straight hair, get a good cut that accentuates the straightness. If you have curly hair, wear it curly. Going natural saves time, money, and energy. If you've been thinking about getting a really short haircut, do it. Most short cuts look great with little or no fuss.

❶ When you are faced with a task you dislike, break it down into **smaller tasks.** Getting a small amount done in several spurts will make the chore much more pleasant.

Limit the number of choices you have to make on a daily basis. Pare down your wardrobe to your favorite outfits. Plan weekly meals in advance and post the plan on the refrigerator.

Try to **keep up** with things. Keeping up is a lot easier than catching up.

find your center

☀ **❶** Give your children simple things to do that can help keep the family **organized.** For example, keep a file rack on the kitchen counter or other common area and assign a different color folder to each child into which they are responsible for putting paperwork from school that requires your attention.

As you plan your day and put your plan into action, resist the urge to do just one more thing or buy just one more thing.

If you have trouble making a decision, ASK YOURSELF if it will matter in five years. If it won't, then you can relax in the knowledge that there is more than one "right" decision.

find your center

S-t-r-e-t-c-h. You don't even have to get out of bed to incorporate some **stretching** into your morning routine! Lie on your back and reach your arms up and over your head. With your toes pointing straight up to the ceiling, push out through your heels and reach your fingertips as far back as you can. Really stretch; hold for five seconds and release.

Do it again, but this time stretch only through your right side. Then stretch only through your left side. Stretching circulates the blood to your head to give you a rush of energy to start your day.

find your center

☀ Take a few moments each morning to **center yourself** and think about how you will keep your life in balance today.

☀ If you feel like dancing, move your feet and invite the rest of your body to follow! If you feel like singing, belt out a tune at the top of your lungs!

☀ Smile at everyone you pass today and see how good it feels. Don't be surprised if people **smile** back, which will make you feel doubly good.

find your center

☀ While walking around your neighborhood, driving to work, or just sitting in your backyard, look for something you've never noticed before. There is a simple but profound pleasure in **discovery.**

☀ Yak, yak, yak. Social contact with friends may help keep your heart healthy. Think of face-to-face conversation as an alternative to television.

Always, there will be people with more wealth, charms, and abilities than you — as well as people who have far less than you. BE CONTENT with what you have today.

Accept that you aren't perfect. People will still love you even when you make mistakes. They may even love you more for it. **Accept** that others have shortcomings too. Forgiving others' mistakes heals both parties and frees us to learn from the past and move forward.

Make time for family and friends. Don't double-book yourself.

find your center

Tomorrow is another day. If grief or sorrow, pain or suffering does not allow you to rejoice today, remember that this too shall pass. Every once in a while on our journey, we have to go through a dark tunnel. Challenge yourself to keep moving and eventually you will see the **light** on the other side.

Give yourself a 15-minute time-out every day. Spend it **quietly** doing nothing or doing something that brings you joy.

find your center

Do your best to speak the **truth** about all things. If you have a tendency to tell little white lies (or big, brazen lies), then you have to remember everything you tell everyone. This creates stress and also eats up a lot of energy. Being true to yourself and honest with others will set you free.

Cultivate close friendships. It is better to have one or two really **close friends** than a dozen acquaintances. Good friends are those with whom you can talk about nothing and anything.

We're always so busy planning for the future. But what's the point when you waste the here and now? Don't focus on tomorrow; REJOICE in what you have *today*.

find your center

There's a **whole other world** out there that is moving at the same pace today as it did thousands of years ago. The sun rises each morning with precision and certainty, and sets each evening the same way. When was the last time you watched the sun set or rise?

Tune in to the **sounds** of nature. There's something reassuring and soothing about nature's rhythms.

find your center

Join a bicycling or hiking club and participate in regular outings.

Take nourishment from the **sun.** Just 10 to 15 minutes of direct sun exposure to your face, arms, and hands three times a week stimulates your body to produce all the vitamin D you need.

Learning contributes to our sense of general well-being, perhaps because it helps us better understand ourselves and our world. When you make it a lifelong pursuit, **learning** can help simplify your life by opening your eyes to possibilities you never knew existed.

Read. It's amazing what you can learn by reading — even when you're not actively trying to learn!

Push your limits — physically, socially, emotionally, intellectually, and spiritually — and allow yourself the **opportunity** to discover and appreciate the greatness within you.

find your center

☀ Find the **silver lining.** For every action, there is an equal and opposite reaction. Look for the positive in everything negative that happens in your life.

Keep a "can do" attitude. Two little boys were playing on an oceanside beach when suddenly a large wave rushed over them. When the wave receded, one boy was crying and the other was laughing. They were both hit by the same wave, but each perceived it very differently. Remember, it's not *what* happens to us, but what *attitude* we choose that shapes our experiences.

find your center

Accept **serendipity.** *Webster's* defines *serendipity* as "the finding of valuable or agreeable things not sought for." As you think about what would bring more meaning and satisfaction to your life, pay close attention to what is going on around you. Serendipitous events happen all the time; we just don't always recognize them!

☀ Walk tall. Good posture makes you look better and feel better. So stand up straight, lift your chin so that it's parallel to the floor, tuck in your abdomen and buttocks, and relax your shoulders.

find your center

By taking charge of your thoughts, you can turn them into a powerful source of **inner strength** and confidence. Let's say, for example, that your best friend becomes upset about something you've done. Your initial response is hurt or anger because you think you've done nothing wrong. But then, in reviewing the situation, you discover something about yourself that you decide to change. In this way, you can be thankful for the experience.

Converse with your Higher Power — aloud, or in your head. Ask for help. Pray for the welfare of friends or family. Offer THANKS for the beauty and goodness in the world.

find your center

One way to **simplify** daily living is to open your heart to your community and to your Higher Power. Find meaningful ways to connect with friends and strangers alike. Establishing a link with yourself and others is like feeding your soul.

Be of service. Whether you volunteer for community service projects, help at a school, or visit senior citizens, by giving of your time you help make the world a better place and bring more fulfillment to your own life.

find your center

Spend time with people who support your efforts to live according to your values. Attend services with a community of believers. Look for and attend a Voluntary Simplicity group in your area. Or start your own **support group** or study circle among friends, neighbors, or coworkers.

find your center

A good deed can do wonders for your heart. Try these random acts of kindness:

- **Brush snow off a stranger's car in a parking lot.**

- **Send flowers anonymously to someone who could use a little cheering up.**

- **Leave candies on the chairs of coworkers while they are at lunch.**

- **If someone is waiting to pull out into traffic, let that person go ahead of you.**

- **Pay the toll for the car behind you at a tollbooth.**

- **Leave store coupons near the coupon items on supermarket shelves.**

find your center

❶ Withhold criticism or judgment. The more you refrain from passing judgment on others, the less you will hear yourself.

❶ Appreciate your surroundings. Look for beauty in the people, places, and things that you come into contact with each day.

CHOOSE to be happy.

find your center

☀ Give a **hug,** or ask for one.

Make Sunday (or one day a week) a **day of rest.** Plan to share time with family and friends. Don't feel that you have to do anything special; just be together.

☀ Start a "thanksgiving" journal. Each evening, write down the **good things** that happened throughout your day. Keeping a journal like this helps us to appreciate the many blessings that might otherwise go unnoticed.

PART TWO

Keep Clear

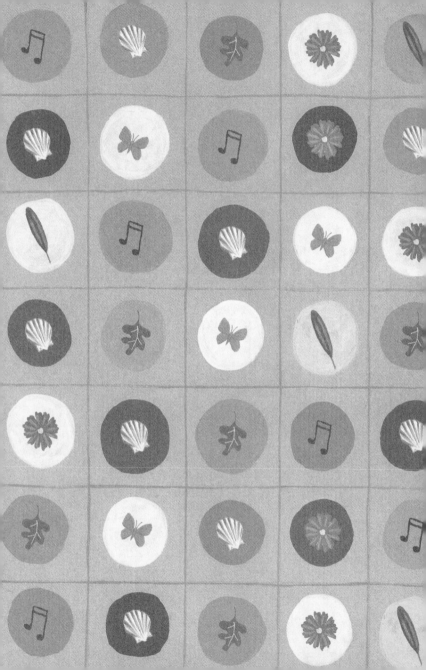

CHAPTER 5

Discover Your Gifts

People who love their work dare to follow their passion. Maybe they knew what they wanted all along — or maybe not.

Sometimes, someone who really enjoys her job is not doing what she initially set out to do. But somehow, she figured out what kind of work would bring her satisfaction.

You, too, are free to discover and pursue what brings a sense of purpose, satisfaction, and happiness to your life. And truly, the only person stopping you is you.

When we were little kids, we thought we could DO ANYTHING and BE ANYBODY when we grew up. Somewhere along the way we lost faith in ourselves.

discover your gifts

Have you ever had a **gut feeling** so strong you just had to go with it? It turned out to be the best thing you could have done, didn't it? Let your instincts guide you.

☀ The next time you start to compare yourself to someone you think is brighter, prettier, worthier, or whatever, stop. You are who you are — a very unique and special individual. **Believe in yourself.** That's all that really matters.

discover your gifts

One of the ways **inner wisdom** speaks to you is through dreams. Sometimes your dreams are your unconscious trying to help you. Look for the helping message in your dreams.

Whether you are trying to lose weight, launch a new career, or save a faltering marriage, try your best. If it doesn't work out, you can be secure in the knowledge that you did everything you could. Nothing worth doing is easy.

❶ **Act as if you can** do whatever you want to do and eventually you will be able to do it.

discover your gifts

☀ Revel in your accomplishments and **accept praise** for a job well done. Really let it sink in and become a part of who you are — don't just brush it off in modesty.

☀ On momentous occasions, write down your thoughts and feelings about your achievements to reread on a day when you're feeling down.

my big day

discover your gifts

Remember the three Rs:

- Respect for self

- Respect for others

- Responsibility for all your actions

Appreciate and accept yourself.
If you do, others will too.

discover your gifts

☀ Keep pushing forward. Don't give up as long as you still have something to give. Nothing is really over until you stop trying.

☀ Don't be afraid to admit a mistake. Being **less than perfect** is the common thread of humanity. When you realize that you've made a mistake, apologize and then take immediate steps to correct it.

☀ Accept your emotions. It's okay to feel sad or angry. It's okay to cry. Part of believing in yourself is accepting your feelings. To deny your feelings is to deny yourself.

discover your gifts

We all are born with special talents or gifts. **Your gifts** might include compassion, humor, insight, or inspiring others. Or you may be a born comedian or a natural peacemaker. In *Live the Life You Love*, Barbara Sher suggests that you think about everything you have ever enjoyed doing: "If you base what you do on your gifts, you will be unusually good at it." Identify your natural gifts — and use them.

discover your gifts

What do you love to do? What makes you happy to be alive? If your time and money were unlimited, and you could do anything you wanted, what would you do? Recognizing the things that give you joy and satisfaction puts you on the path to increased **fulfillment.**

☀ Pretend that you are someone who has just met you. What desirable qualities might this person you've just created see in you?

Don't let others limit you with their expectations. Only you can determine what will bring **joy** to your life.

discover your gifts

Businesspeople often analyze the viability of ideas and develop strategies based on the S.W.O.T. technique. Try it as a tool for assessing your own goals:

- **Strengths.** What strengths do you possess that will enable you to succeed? List your talents and skills.

- **Weaknesses.** Identify your weaknesses. What can you do to shore up these weaknesses? Develop and implement a plan of action.

- **Opportunities.** What is going on in the world around you? Can you see any trends? Where is the greatest need for your expertise or talent?

- **Threats.** What obstacles stand in your way? How big a threat are these obstacles to your success? What can you do to minimize or steer around these obstacles?

discover your gifts

Don't confuse skills with talents. You may have learned how to do your current job very well, but that doesn't mean it's what you want to do. If you do a job because that's what you know how to do and not because you want to do it, you are likely to be very unhappy.

discover your gifts

What did you want to be when you grew up? What kind of response did you get from your elders? Often, we don't pursue our original passion because of negative feedback we received.

For example, you might have wanted to be an astronaut, but your parents told you that you didn't do well enough in science or math. What if your dream was to be a superhero? Well, obviously you can't become a comic-book hero. Did you like the thought of rescuing people from danger or simply helping them? There are many ways to live a **life of service.**

Close your eyes and visualize yourself working at your DREAM job.

discover your gifts

One idea from Joyce Chapman's book *Live Your Dream* is to cut out magazine pictures and words, use photos, or draw illustrations that portray your dream of who you want to be. Include the aspects of life such as family, friends, and accomplishments that are important to you. In essence, what you design is an advertisement for the life you want to live. Put this **dream board** where you will see it every day.

Allowing yourself to follow your true passion will not only enhance your life, it will also give you the sense of ACCOMPLISHMENT.

discover your gifts

Look for career opportunities that use your **inherent skills.** If you are a natural problem-solver, for instance, make up a list of occupations that require problem-solving. Yes, it's going to be a long list!

Spend some time visualizing yourself in each one of these occupations. Do any of them excite you? Spend a few days or more "noodling" with the idea of this or that career. Then start researching what kind of qualifications you will need for the careers that most appeal to you.

discover your gifts

To get through the front door, you may need specific education and experience. But if you're lacking these, don't despair. Perhaps there is a side door. Identify the industry in which you wish to work. Is there another job within that field for which you may be qualified? Once you are there, you can take the **necessary steps** to prove yourself.

Rewrite your résumé to call attention to your natural talents. Redefine what you want in your next job, and then describe your experience in a way that highlights your natural gifts and supports your objective.

discover your gifts

Perhaps your **dream job** is not as far away as you think. If you are currently employed, is there some way of altering or adding to your current job responsibilities to make better use of your talents while still serving your employer?

☀ Know that every action, every step you take is bringing you one step closer to your dream career.

Don't waste your life waiting for the **perfect moment** to begin something you want to do. The perfect time is now.

People who do what they LOVE quickly discover that the money becomes a by-product of their passion.

discover your gifts

In *Life Mapping*, author Bill Cohen suggests dividing your goals into a list of activities necessary to **complete those goals.** Keep breaking them into smaller and smaller activities, until each individual activity can be completed within a week or a day. Put the list in chronological order. Then get going on what you need to do this week.

If you dread doing some of the things on your goals list, try to make them fun. Bill Cohen suggests, for example, that if you have to call a long list of people, try to make each of them laugh.

discover your gifts

Write down 100 things you'd like to do before you die. Identify the top 10 and work them into your **goals.** Then determine which ones you want to accomplish this year.

Let's say you want to start your own business. One **challenge** you face is saving enough money to quit your job. You've been trying, but there is never enough left over at the end of the month. Try paying yourself first. Out of each paycheck set aside a sum of money for yourself. By securing it for yourself, you are securing your future.

discover your gifts

Talk to people who are doing what you want to do. **Ask** them how they got started, what they think it takes to succeed in this business, and anything else you want to know about their work lives.

Many senior-level individuals are willing to make time for people who take the initiative to seek them out. Start by **offering** to buy lunch for that person. Use this time to present one or two of your ideas or challenges. Then **listen** to the voice of experience.

discover your gifts

One of the best and quickest ways to gain experience and make yourself known is to offer your services on a **volunteer** basis. Organizations are *always* looking for people who are willing to help! For example, if you want to get involved in politics, join an election committee. Not only will you get experience, you also will meet the "movers and shakers" in your intended line of work.

discover your gifts

Read every book you can find on the subject of your passion. Take a crash course. **Research** the industry. Talk to experts.

Following your passion may be a stretch — financially, emotionally, physically, and intellectually — but it should never require you to compromise your values. If something doesn't feel right, it's not right for you. Walk away.

discover your gifts

If you want to **change careers,** do something every day to work toward achieving your goal of a new career. Make a phone call. Write a letter. Practice your craft. Network.

You've identified your talents. You've found your **true calling.** You've researched the best way to pursue it. So what's holding you back? Fear and uncertainty are usually the main obstacles on the road to self-fulfillment. Just remember that there is nothing wrong with being afraid — but you *can* learn to overcome this feeling.

discover your gifts

① What's the worst possible thing that could happen? This is an excellent question to ask yourself when you are faced with a difficult decision or you are afraid to do something.

If you're scared, do it scared! We're all afraid of doing things we've never done before; it's only natural. Here's a little **secret:** Once you do it, you won't be so afraid the second time around.

discover your gifts

If you can't muster enough **courage** or if you need more preparation before you try, take it a step at a time. For example, if you want to become writer, set aside at least 15 minutes a day to write. It doesn't matter what you write, and it doesn't have to be good. After a month or two, select something you've written and submit it to a magazine or publisher. If it gets rejected, don't take it personally. Remember, all good writers were **beginners** at one time, and most of them still have the rejection letters to prove it!

Worry about today's problems, not tomorrow's. REMEMBER the old southern expression: Don't worry that the mule is blind — just load the wagon.

discover your gifts

Write down stumbling blocks that are keeping you from pursuing your dream. Now ask yourself, "Is this within my power to change? What could I do to change this?" Write down every answer you can think of, including outrageous answers like "win the lottery" and "have my own talk show."

Pick one that you can start working on today, and work on it every day. Achieving your dream is like trying to move a large boulder down hill. It's hard work to get it rolling, but once it starts, it quickly gathers **momentum.**

discover your gifts

You fell down the first time you tried to walk, but you didn't let that stop you from **trying again.** Were you able to swim or ride a bike on your first try? Probably not. In failing, we learn what doesn't work, which frees us to try various other approaches that might work. The only real failure is not trying at all.

discover your gifts

Live Your Dream author Joyce Chapman suggests listing 20 habits and/or **beliefs** that you allow to stand in the way of achieving your dream. Procrastination and over-committing are two examples of dream-defeating *habits;* believing that you're not qualified enough or smart enough is a dream-defeating *belief.*

Next to each item on your list, write a new **habit** or belief to replace the old one. You might also want to include on your list people who stand in your way, but instead of replacing them, consider how you might modify your relationship with them.

discover your gifts

It's only natural to have some doubts and concerns about following **your passion,** particularly if it means changing careers and *especially* if you have a family to support.

Think you're too old or it's too late? Apparently Grandma Moses thought differently. She began painting in her late 70s. Think you don't have time to pursue your passion? You can always make time for what's really important by spending less time on less important things.

When you lose, don't lose the lesson. LEARN from your mistakes.

discover your gifts

For some people, self-employment is only a dream. Others find the courage to try it, but discover that they were happier with a steady paycheck. Still others couldn't imagine ever going back to a regular job. **Careful thought** can help you determine if it's right for you.

Some say that you should start your own business when you have so much money that it doesn't matter if you lose it — or when you have so little, there's nothing to lose. But don't let money be the deciding factor.

discover your gifts

Make sure you understand the realities of self-employment. For example, working for yourself often means working *by* yourself, and that can get pretty lonely. It also requires a tremendous amount of self-discipline. You've got to get up and get going every day. The more you can stick to a **regular routine,** the more successful you are likely to be.

✹ Be honest with yourself. How much time are you willing to commit? What are you willing to do? What are you willing to give up and for how long?

discover your gifts

If you say that you want your own business but never do anything about it, what does that tell you? Is it really what you want? If so, take **action.** If not, figure out what you find appealing about self-employment. For example, if you like the idea of having more freedom, perhaps you can negotiate to work at home one day a week.

discover your gifts

Before you quit your day job, try starting your business on a part-time or **freelance** basis. It's a great way to get a feel for the marketplace and learn what challenges there are to finding work.

Talk to people who are currently self-employed to find out if self-employment is right for you.

discover your gifts

If your passion is to be at home with your children, but you need to supplement your family income, ask yourself:

Is the work I do now something I could do from home?

Do I have a professional skill such as writing, typing, accounting, or bookkeeping that could be promoted as a service?

Can I turn a hobby or a talent into an income producer?

discover your gifts

Don't think that just because you're in business, customers are going to come knocking on your door. There are many excellent books on ways to **promote** your business on a shoestring budget. One of the best ways to get your name known is to volunteer your expertise in a high-profile position in one or more industry or trade associations. Also, look for networking organizations through which members regularly meet to share leads.

discover your gifts

Working for yourself usually means that you are also the secretary, bookkeeper, salesperson, and janitor. Consider taking a course or reading up on time-management techniques.

When starting a business, it's always a good idea to have enough money in the bank to cover your expenses for at least six months. Also have a **backup plan** (such as waiting on tables, housecleaning, or temporary work) that will allow you to earn enough to pay the bills.

There's only ONE person who can make you successful and happy, and that's you.

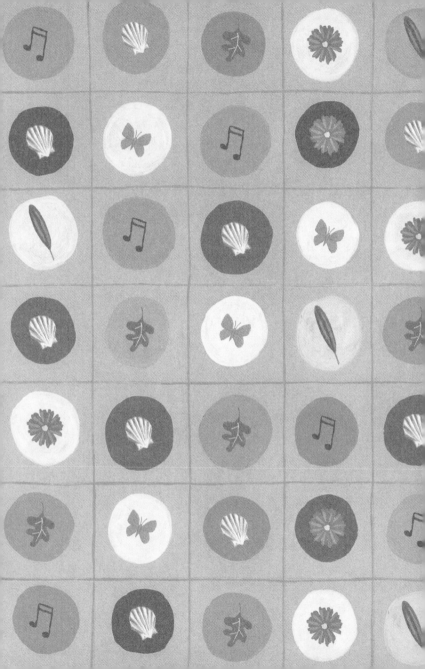

CHAPTER 6

Lighten Your Load

What are your beliefs about money? How much money is enough? Many people are discovering that less is more. The less you spend, the less you need to work. And the less you have to work, the more time you have for the things that really matter.

Money may be at the heart of your cluttered life. Although you may never achieve financial independence, you can keep clear of financial worries by reducing debt (and spending) and increasing savings. That's financial freedom.

lighten your load

The best way to figure out where your money goes is to keep track of every penny you spend for an entire month. Fill out a form each week for one month and then total what you spent in each category. Once you know where all your money is going, you can develop a **realistic budget** that is much easier to maintain.

RESIST the urge
to have immediate
gratification.

Once you have established a realistic budget, make a conscientious effort to stick to it for at least three months. At the end of each month, compare your budget figures to actual figures. If you are way off course after the first month, see if you can **make adjustments** during the next month to bring those numbers closer together.

Shopping for a car? Consider a good used car instead of a new car. Use the money you saved with a lower car payment to reduce debt or add to your **savings.**

lighten your load

Create separate envelopes for groceries, gas, entertainment, and other regularly occurring **expenses.** Each week, put into these envelopes the cash amount you have budgeted for each expense.

Automatic teller machines (ATMs) are a wonderfully convenient way to access your money, but ATM fees can add up. Make it a point to use ATMs that do not charge you for your own money.

lighten your load

Look at your spending over the past week. Where might you be able to cut back on spending without affecting the quality of your life? Many people spend $5 a day or more on lunches. That's $1,300 a year! You could save money by bringing your lunch from home.

Look for **"cash cushions."** Money above and beyond the amount needed to pay monthly bills and expenses often gets frittered away. Use it toward debt reduction or savings.

lighten your load

Arrange for automatic transfers from your paycheck to an investment or savings account. Doing this will give you more security and, ultimately, **financial freedom.**

☀ ❶ Know the difference between wants and needs. We *need* food, water, shelter, and clothing. We *want* gourmet meals, big-screen televisions, fancy cars, and stylish apparel. Before you go shopping for a particular item, ask yourself whether it is something you need or something you want. If it's luxury item and you really "must" have it, develop a budget for it.

lighten your load

If credit cards are a necessity, choose cards that pay you to use them. Some credit cards offer rewards or **cash back** on total annual purchases. If you use it for everything (groceries, gas, restaurants, travel, and so on), you get back a little something every year to add to your savings or investment fund.

The key is to **pay off your balance** every month; otherwise the interest you pay will far outweigh the cash you get back. And be sure to choose a card that does not charge an annual fee.

lighten your load

If you can, pay bills as they come in. That way, you won't have to think about them, and you won't forget to pay them on time.

Fill a three-ring binder with 12 pocket folders for filing receipts and bills each month. You can easily keep track of payments by writing the check number, amount, and date paid on each folder. This method is especially handy if you have a lot of household expenses that are tax deductible, because you'll have everything in one place when tax time rolls around.

lighten your load

☀️ **❶** Look at the real cost of your purchases. Calculate how many hours you need to work to pay for each item you want to buy.

Trade credit cards for debit cards. A debit card combines the **convenience** of a credit card with the **sensibility** of paying cash. Debit cards are different from credit cards, as they are tied to cash in a bank account. They are particularly useful because they keep you from spending more than you have.

When you shop with cash, you don't have to spend any time wondering if you can really AFFORD something: Either you have enough cash or you don't.

lighten your load

Here's a foolproof plan for getting rid of credit card debt:

1. List debts in order of the lowest to highest amounts owed. Use the money you have freed up by budgeting to pay extra toward the first debt on your list.

2. Pay the minimum amount due on the other debts. Follow this practice each month until the first debt on your list is paid.

3. Combine the amount you've been paying on the first debt to the minimum monthly amount due on the next debt until it, too, is paid. Continue until all debt is paid.

4. Apply your total debt reduction payment each month to savings and investments.

lighten your load

If you make even one late payment or skip a payment one month, many credit card companies will increase your interest rate dramatically. If you must, make a late payment to a more lenient creditor such as the telephone or electric company.

Filing for bankruptcy may seem like an easy out, but a bankruptcy remains on your credit report for 10 years and may affect your ability to **secure** a loan for a car or home. It also may rear its ugly head in a routine employment check and cost you a job.

lighten your load

Pay attention to notices on your bill. Some credit companies will try to raise your interest rate for no reason at all. But they are required by law to notify you in advance and give you the option of declining the higher rate of interest.

Pare down to one credit card.

lighten your load

If you are paying on a credit card or loan, you may receive credit checks from time to time with an enticement to use them to go on a well-deserved vacation, install a backyard pool for some summer-time fun, or simply give yourself a nice cash bonus. Don't do it; it's a debt trap.

Don't try ducking creditors. You'll buy yourself more time if you settle on an amount and show that you are willing to **repay** your debt. If you are having difficulty making minimum payments, contact the Consumer Credit Counseling Service in your area.

lighten your load

❶ Freeze your credit — literally. If you tend to overspend on credit, put your credit cards in a small plastic tub filled with water and place the tub in the freezer. Freezing your credit cards will curb impulse credit card shopping by helping you make a **conscious choice** about what and when you will buy on credit. Once you get used to buying with cash (and you see your credit card balances going down), you may want to cut up those credit cards. (Thaw them first!)

lighten your load

It's a good idea to cancel credit cards that are paid in full for two reasons. First, it will keep you from getting sucked back into charging. Second, the credit card companies will notify the credit reporting agencies and your credit file will be updated. This is important because having too much open credit could result in a loan denial for a major purchase such as a home or car.

You don't need to make more money to REDUCE your debt. You simply need to change what you do with the money you have.

lighten your load

- ☀ If you're short one month, you may be tempted to take a cash advance on one credit card to pay the monthly payment due on another card. Don't do it! You're digging yourself deeper into debt.

Use automatic payments from your paycheck (or checking or savings account) to fund investment contributions and **learn to live** on what's left rather than overspending and finding yourself unable to make regular contributions.

lighten your load

If you've got a steady job, chances are very good that you're spending money as fast as you earn it, and that you have a hard time keeping yourself from dipping into your savings for this and that. You might not be worried now about what you're going to live on when you **retire,** but the sooner you start putting money away, the more money you'll have later.

lighten your load

Consider moving money from traditional savings and money market accounts to certificates of deposit. A certificate of deposit allows you to deposit a certain amount of money as an investment for a fixed length of time. CDs are federally insured and pay much **higher rates** of return.

❶ Before you write out checks for bills, make a payment to a savings or investment account.

lighten your load

Live within your means by using the 70-20-10 rule. Use 70 percent of your take-home pay for regular monthly bills plus other regular expenses such as groceries, gas, and clothing. Set aside 20 percent for large-ticket items such as a car or home. Save the remaining 10 percent. Following this rule will help keep you from overextending yourself with credit.

lighten your load

The U.S. government allows a tax deduction when you invest in a traditional or Roth Individual Retirement Account (IRA). The earlier you start investing, the more your investment will grow. Check with your tax specialist to learn about options, restrictions, and eligibility requirements.

If your company offers a 401K program, take full advantage of it. Automatic deductions from your paycheck make it a painless way to save for retirement. Some companies even offer to match part of your contribution, which really helps your balance grow.

lighten your load

-☀- ❶- Plan to **invest** any extra cash that comes your way rather than spend it.

Ask family members to think of ways they can **save money** each week. Keep a chart of the money saved so that you can monitor your progress. Offer a reward such as a family trip for reaching the goal.

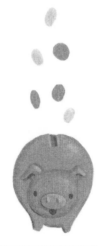

lighten your load

Look at the little picture. Let's say, for example, that you want to save $2,000 over the next year. That works out to $5.48 a day. Now look at your daily expenses. Where might you be able to cut back by $5.48 each day? **Start putting away** that amount — in cash — every day. At the end of the week, take your saved money to the bank and deposit it to your savings account.

❶ Get into the habit — and encourage family members to get in the habit — of putting all loose change in a jar every night. At the end of the week, roll up your change and deposit it in your savings account.

If you are struggling to make ends meet, you can RECLAIM control over your finances — and your LIFE — by choosing to consume less.

lighten your load

When you eat out, you have to add an extra 15 to 20 percent to the bill for service, and you pay a ridiculous price for beverages. If you enjoy going out to eat but don't enjoy paying the high price of a gourmet dinner, go out for a gourmet brunch or lunch instead for about **half the price** — or less.

Too tired to cook at night? Cook large meals on the weekends and eat leftovers during the week.

lighten your load

Buy canned food and paper products in **bulk.** Store them in your basement or garage (providing they are dry), out of the reach of potential pests.

Grow a vegetable **garden.** Plan meals around what's in season. Trade produce with neighbors and coworkers.

☼ Eating meat less often will reduce your food bill considerably. Substitute main dishes that feature eggs, beans, cheese, or tofu as a source of protein.

lighten your load

Take care of what you own. When you buy items, choose high quality over low price. High-quality, high-efficiency, **durable goods** will last longer and can be repaired if necessary.

Donate clothes to charity and deduct the expense from your income taxes. Or, if they are in excellent condition and relatively new or classically styled, get cash by selling them at a consignment shop. Make even more money by picking up good, cheap clothes at yard sales and selling them on consignment.

lighten your load

If you have one car that is not driven every day, **compare** the cost of owning a car with the cost of renting a car or taking a cab on the occasions when you need a vehicle.

☀ ❶ Look at the many things you own. Do you wear all of your jewelry and clothes? Probably not. Do you use all the gadgets in your kitchen? Probably not. Do you have more material possessions than your parents and grandparents did? Probably. Be thankful for the **abundance** in your life.

Buy only out of need, such as to REPLACE something that is used up, worn out, or broken beyond repair.

lighten your load

Buy greeting cards, wrapping paper, and seasonal decorations at half price right after the holidays. For very inexpensive gifts, look for new items at online auction sites, garage sales, secondhand stores, consignment shops, and thrift shops. Or start early and make your own gifts.

Shop with a list and stick to what's on your list. If you see something else you want, resist the urge to buy it on the spot. Go home and think about it for a few days and then decide if it's worth going back for.

lighten your load

If you can **do your own repairs** or make things you normally buy, you can save money. Perhaps you know someone willing to teach you what you need to learn. Or your local high school or community college may offer skills-based continuing education classes.

☀ Rent movies instead of going to the movie theater.

Keep track of your member discounts from organizations and associations — and use them.

lighten your load

Take advantage of off-peak discounts. Some museums offer free admission on certain days. Look for early-bird dinner specials. Attend matinees instead of prime-time movies and save cash. Buy movie tickets in bulk. Many movie theater chains offer tickets by mail, which sell at about 40 percent off the regular price.

lighten your load

Scan local newspapers and community bulletin boards to find low- or no-cost activities in your area. There are numerous opportunities out there. All it takes is a little creative thinking and the desire to have fun for **free!**

Go to your nearest visitors center and pick up local-interest brochures or ask about **fun things** to do. Choose places and activities that are new to you.

If you enjoy entertaining but want to keep the cost down, invite friends to a potluck dinner party.

Tune out commercial messages to PROTECT yourself — advertising creates desire.

lighten your load

Visit your local **libraries** and bookstores. Both offer a variety of programs and services that are free and open to the public, including:

- Free Internet access

- Writing workshops

- How-to demonstrations and mini seminars

- Book and poetry readings

- Book discussion groups

- Special-interest exhibits

- Free DVD- and audiocassette loans

- Special-interest discussions

- Magazine swaps

lighten your load

Trade babysitting services. Make arrangements ahead of time to have your **children** spend the night with friends or family members, with the understanding that you will take in their children another night.

Vacation at home. It's simpler, less expensive, and can be far more relaxing than jetting (or driving) to and from a vacation destination. Create an itinerary just as you would for a regular vacation. Plan to see the local sights that visitors come to see. Try out a new restaurant or two. Leave housework for when you "get back." You're on vacation!

lighten your load

If you **plan a trip** to an amusement park or other venue that charges exorbitant prices for food and beverages, don't blow your hard-earned money on expensive drinks and snacks. Load a child's wagon with a small cooler and tow it along with you. If there's enough room, young children can ride in the wagon when they get tired.

Take a walk — and **talk.** Sure, the exercise will do you all good, but the most important benefit of this activity is that it allows you to give your kids what they crave more than anything — your attention.

lighten your load

Following are some ideas for slowing down the pace with some simple, old-fashioned family fun:

- **Pick your own apples or berries.**
- **Bake cookies or cupcakes.**
- **Play board games.**
- **Go fly a kite.**
- **Build a fort — indoors or outdoors.**
- **Have a neighborhood sidewalk-drawing contest.**
- **Take a family bike ride.**
- **Bring a picnic lunch to the beach.**
- **Rent a rowboat on a nearby lake.**
- **Schedule a family reading hour.**
- **Put on a play or skit.**

lighten your load

Let your kids camp out in the back-yard for **memories** that will last a lifetime.

Plant a vegetable garden. Kids love to watch things grow, especially if they have a hand in planting and caring for them.

❶ When kids get bored, their **imaginations** kick in and they come up with truly creative ways to entertain themselves. Let your children get bored once in a while, and see what happens!

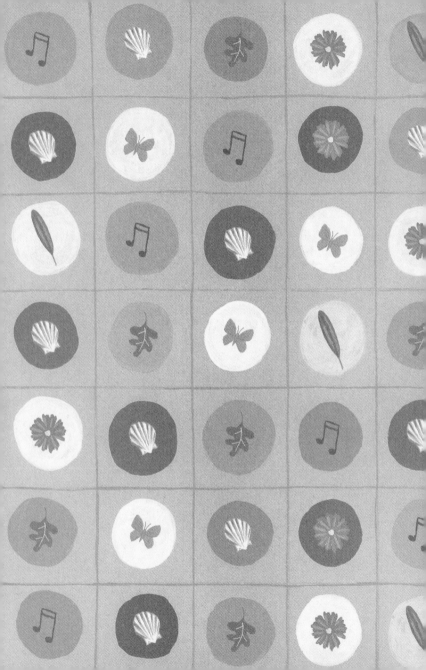

CHAPTER 7

Learn to Let Go

Into each life, a little clutter must fall. But you don't have to hold on to it forever! If your life feels out of balance, you can free up time, space, and energy for more important things.

Start by paring down your possessions to those things you either love or use regularly. Minimizing stress will lighten your mind; lighten your heart by letting go of guilt, anger, and other negative emotions and adding more humor and laughter. You'll be healthier and happier for it.

learn to let go

How much is **enough?** Do you really need 23 pairs of shoes? Or seven sets of sheets for your bed? Or that handy-dandy gadget you just saw advertised on television? How many things that you have bought are still in your home but not being used?

Acquiring things has become such a habit that we often don't consider the **cost of acquisition.** Material possessions cost you storage space, and they cost you the time it takes to shop and care for them. The more you own, the more you have to care for.

BETTER to have a few possessions that you love and use than a thousand that weigh you down.

learn to let go

Do not try to **unclutter** your whole home all at once. Work in one room at a time and don't switch to another room until you're done. Seeing **progress** will motivate you to keep up the good work.

Clean out one drawer each night.

Plan uncluttering activities around garbage days or plan to take stuff to the dump or your selected charity that day. Otherwise, you may be tempted to reconsider.

learn to let go

Start uncluttering with the easy stuff. Throw out anything that is clearly garbage:

- **Expired medicines and coupons**

- **Outdated clothes and odd socks**

- **Makeup and sunscreen that's more than one year old**

- **Things that are broken (unless they are valuable and fixable)**

- **Grocery bags (10 is probably plenty!)**

- **Old restaurant and shopping guides**

- **Outdated calendars**

- **Spoiled food**

- **Rusted utensils and tools**

- **Travel literature and maps**

- **Refrigerator items past their "use by" date**

learn to let go

Sort belongings into three categories: what you definitely use, what you definitely don't use, and things you can't separate into either of those categories. Put away the things you use. Give away the things you don't use. Store in boxes those things you probably don't use but can't part with just yet. If in six months you haven't opened your boxes, give the items away.

learn to let go

As you decide the **relative merit** of each item you might clear out of your life, ask yourself the following questions:

When was the last time I used this?

Why don't I use it more often?

Does it have any sentimental value?

Do I love it?

Can I live with throwing it away?

Can I get another one if I need to?

If I keep it, where should it go?

How many of these do I need?

learn to let go

❶ Designate one room or space for all papers. This is where you pay bills and file them.

Determine what records you need for tax purposes or other legal reasons and let go of the rest. For your own protection, be sure to destroy any papers that contain personal information — shred them or tear them into tiny pieces.

learn to let go

Technology has changed the way we live, work, interact, and even think. We are bombarded with voice mail, e-mail, and media messages, and it has become increasingly difficult to wade through the clutter to **determine** what's really important. Lightening your load also means making conscious choices about the impact of technology on your life and your environment.

learn to let go

☀ **Assess the worth** of gadgets and appliances in your kitchen. An electric mixer may be easier to use than a wooden spoon, but the spoon is easier to wash. An electric can opener is a convenience, but no use in the event of a power outage.

Put your television in a storage closet for one full week. What did you do with the time you would have spent watching television?

☀ Turn off the ringer on your telephone. When you don't wish to be interrupted, let your answering machine or voice mail service answer calls.

learn to let go

Don't throw out your outdated computer equipment — **donate or recycle** it.

Consider buying computer printer ink in bulk and refilling cartridges. It keeps a lot of packaging out of our landfills and saves 80 to 90 percent of the cost of packaged cartridges.

For a peaceful evening, **unplug** the television, turn off the cellular phone, pager, computer, and fax machine, and turn down the volume on the answering machine.

learn to let go

Does having a cell phone simplify or complicate your life? What **benefit** do you derive from having a cell phone? What's the downside? Can you justify your bill? If you own your own cell phone, you may be able to cancel your contract but still continue using the phone for 911 calls.

☀ Here's a sobering fact: If you chat while you drive, the chances of having an accident are about the same as if you were drunk. If you must make a call from your car, pull over.

Less clutter equals
LESS STRESS.

learn to let go

We can't prevent stress altogether, but with practice, we can moderate or change our reaction to stress so that once-tense situations are far **less stressful** or no longer stressful at all.

Recognize the emotional and physical clues that plague you when under stress: tight upper back, diarrhea or heartburn, craving for carbohydrates, skin problems, forgetfulness, mental fuzziness, bumping into things. When you get the distress signal — whatever it is — don't ignore it.

learn to let go

☀ What's bothering you? An upcoming event? A family problem? A potential layoff at work? Is there something you can do about it? Identify some possible solutions. Then work on a plan. Get whatever help you need and then take action.

☀ You may not be able to control what is causing you stress, but you can change your reaction to it. Look for whatever **humor** may be present. Has a "comedy of errors" led you to your present circumstances? Imagine that you are a stand-up comedian explaining your situation or predicament.

learn to let go

Create a **sacred place.** This can be as simple as a corner of your bedroom with a throw pillow and candle on the floor or as elaborate as a room or an entire house designed using the principles of feng shui. What you want to create is a quiet, peaceful place in which you can close your eyes and shut out the "busyness" of the world around you.

Spend time with people who make you laugh. When choosing which movies to see, choose **comedies** over tragedies. Read the comic strips in your daily newspaper.

learn to let go

Research shows that people who have **family and friends** to help them through stressful times stay healthier and recover faster than those who do not have a social support system.

❶ Slow down. Focus on the quality of your life instead of on doing more and getting ahead.

Find a creative outlet. Draw or paint. Make a birthday card with pictures and letters cut out of magazines. Grow a garden. Write a poem or a letter — to someone else, or perhaps to yourself.

learn to let go

Cultivate **healthy habits** *before* you feel stressed. Quit smoking. Exercise regularly. Limit consumption of alcohol. Eat a balanced diet that's rich in fruits and vegetables. These simple practices will help your body cope with the physical changes brought on by stress.

learn to let go

Meditate stress away. Just sit in a chair and close your eyes. **Visualize** a rope with many knots being lowered slowly into a large body of water and one by one, the knots disappear as you repeat the phrase "Relax . . . let go."

Develop an arsenal of stress techniques that work for you. Simple **breathing** techniques, for example, can keep you from blowing your top in a meeting. Vigorous exercise after work can help you let go of the day's frustrations.

You can't please every-one. But you can PLEASE yourself.

learn to let go

Yoga is the 5,000-year-old remedy for stress. It's an integrated practice of gentle stretching, physical postures, breathing exercises, relaxation techniques, and meditation that can help **reduce stress,** renew energy, and produce a sense of well-being.

Research suggests that sleep deprivation boosts levels of stress-related hormones, like adrenaline, which in turn increases the risk of hypertension, stroke, and other cardiovascular problems. **Sleep** deficiency is also associated with lowered immunity to illness and disease.

learn to let go

Tips for a better night's sleep:

- Go to bed at a regular time each night and set your alarm for the same time every morning to establish a regular sleep schedule.

- Avoid tea, coffee, cola, and cocoa before bed.

- Eat dinner three to four hours before bed to allow time for digestion.

- Exercise every day — earlier, rather than later.

- Use your bedroom primarily for sleeping.

- Avoid or limit daytime naps.

- Listen to relaxation tapes to fall asleep.

- If you can't fall asleep within 15 minutes, get up and do something until you feel sleepy.

learn to let go

-☀- ❶ Caution! If you are under stress, you are also likely to be distracted. Remind yourself to really **focus** on difficult tasks during stressful times. In particular, drive extra carefully or have someone else drive.

learn to let go

It makes sense that when we're feeling happy and peaceful, we want to hold on to our happiness or peaceful state forever. But why are we so reluctant to let go of unhappy emotions?

Letting go doesn't mean suppressing emotions; that's like putting an adhesive bandage on a serious wound. Sure, you can't see it when you cover it up, but it's still festering underneath the bandage. And it just keeps getting worse.

The same is true for emotional wounds. It's important to air negative feelings and mistakes — then let them go so that you can heal.

learn to let go

☀ Anger is a defense mechanism in response to a perceived danger or threat. When you are angry, try to see what's frightening you. If someone is angry with you, try to figure out what might be frightening that person. The best thing you can do is to show **compassion.**

☀ People often say, "Things happen for a reason." When something upsetting happens, think about why it happened to you and why it happened at this particular time in your life. What have you **learned or gained** from this experience?

Don't get even; get angry. Let it all out and then LET IT GO.

learn to let go

1 Until you can **forgive** what happened in the past, you cannot live freely and joyfully in the present. Don't waste another second of precious life imprisoned in the past; forgive and forget, or at least forgive and move on.

Articulate a "taboo" or fear and then break it. For instance, if you've never gone to the movies alone, try it. If you are afraid of a particular item or activity, read up on the subject and then look for an **opportunity** to be exposed to your fear — without fearing for your safety.

learn to let go

❶ Many aspects of everyday living are serious, but that doesn't mean you can't look for the humor in life. Allow yourself to **enjoy** your family, friends, and surroundings, and your life will be all the richer for it.

Guarantee **more fun** in your life. Put yourself in situations and in the company of people you enjoy.

Take time to **play.** If you're walking past a playground, stop and swing awhile. Or take a trip down the slide.

learn to let go

☀️ **❶** When in doubt, **laugh.** Let it out. A good belly laugh not only feels good, but it also gives your abdominal muscles a good workout, easing tension and stress.

Learn to **roll with the punches.** Think of someone you know who always seems to be happy, no matter what happens. There's something he or she is doing that's different from what you are doing in response to life's twists and turns. See if you can figure out what it is. Or ask, "What's your secret?"

learn to let go

❶ Don't take yourself so seriously. Make a **funny face** in the mirror. Now make a *really* funny face.

Spare yourself the clutter caused by bad feelings. **Participate** in activities that make you feel good; eliminate or reduce your participation in activities that don't.

Double your happiness: Share it!

learn to let go

❶ Go with the flow. Being **flexible** allows greater enjoyment of today. An appointment that gets canceled, for example, is an opportunity to enjoy some unexpected free time.

Sing and dance away negative emotions. In using voice and movement, we free negative energy that is stored within our bodies. Try it next time you are home alone. Put on your favorite **music** and sing and dance to it. If you've got a good imagination, pretend that you're a famous performer in front of a very receptive audience.

learn to let go

When you are faced with one of life's lessons in patience, such as a traffic jam or a long line at the checkout, remember that while you may have no control over the situation, your **attitude** is within your control. You can choose to be angry and frustrated, or you can choose to be calm and relaxed. Strike up a conversation with a stranger. Or entertain yourself by looking at the people around you and making up stories about their lives.

learn to let go

-✸- If it is difficult for you to let go of negative emotions, create an **affirmation** to help you. Your affirmation might be something like "I am a loving, forgiving person" or "My heart radiates the healing energy of forgiveness." Repeat your affirmation aloud a few times every day.

-✸- Rate upsetting or annoying events on a scale of one to ten. Save your energy for the truly big stuff.

learn to let go

Try turning the television on a half hour later than usual or turning it off a half hour earlier, and then take that time to do something else. Better yet, don't turn the television on.

Eliminate one activity that you do on a regular basis that provides you with little or no **satisfaction** and only adds to your sense of being overwhelmed.

Think of procrastination as a thief that steals YOUR TIME.

learn to let go

Include on your "to do" list a realistic **estimate** of the time you will need to complete that activity or task. This will keep you from over-committing.

☀ ❶ Plan time to do things that give you joy, such as spending time with your children, visiting friends and family, or gardening. Then **schedule** everything else around that time. Why should it be the reverse?

learn to let go

Delegate anything on your "to do" list that can be delegated and simply cross off those items that have been on your list forever. If you're doing more than your fair share of work around the house, ask other household members which tasks they would be willing to pick up.

Whether you're trying to unclutter a closet or write up a report at work, keep at it until the job is done.

Politely **excuse yourself** from involvement with various committees and boards that are creating any undue stress.

Don't waste time try-ing to change things over which you have no control. ACCEPT the things you cannot change and move on.

learn to let go

☀ Don't let **guilt** make you take on more than you can handle. Just say no.

☀ At the end of the day, look back on your uncompleted tasks. Why where they left uncompleted? What held you up? How can you make sure they get done the next day?

If it's safe, **encourage children** who are old enough to walk, bike, or skate to school and to after-school activities — or use public transportation so that you're not spending so much time in the car shuttling kids.

learn to let go

1 Nobody's going to die if you don't get everything on your list done today. **Remind yourself** every once in a while that all you really must do is breathe in and breathe out.

index